MW01235763

This book is dedicated to

God and all of His Angels
my parents, Sue and Robert
my children, Deanna and Patrick
Summer, my friend
& Donna Rhose,
a very special earth angel

Angel
Messages
from Penny

by Penny Spezzano

ISBN 978-1-4357-2912-4
lulu.com

The Rhose Connection
www.RhoseConnection.com/angel

Suggestions on how
to use this book

Angel Messages from Penny
can be used

For a daily meditation.

Opened to a page for a message.

*To help you with guidance
for the day.*

*To help you with inspiration
of the moment.*

*To use as a tool to communicate
with your Angels.*

SPIRITUAL PRACTICAL TOOLS

Nobody taught me how to get close to God, not really. I can say that my Angels helped me with finding my way to God. They lit the path and dropped breadcrumbs along the way for me to follow.

So, I had to teach myself. I guess that is what I am, self-taught.

It is a process, a changing of one's patterns and habits. To go within.

To be able to do this, I would first have to get my mind back because it is something I gave away a long time ago. I allowed it to wander around haphazardly without any responsibility to me. I was not present with it. Taking responsibility for one's self is a great responsibility and would take a lot of awareness on my part. That means, I would have to answer to myself and for myself.

Each morning I would do a visual exercise for myself. I would put out my right hand in front of my face and take the other hand and lift it up to my head. I would verbally speak to God and recite these words with hand gestures. With my left hand I would move it back and forth from my head to my other hand saying. 'I am removing all doubt, guilt, fear and judgment from my head'. I just emptied out my head and put all the negative stuff in my right hand. Boy, did my hand get heavy. I just emptied out my head. All those things in my hand are the things I allowed to sit in the God Throne. None of the things I removed are of God, yet I spend so much time worshipping and practicing that stuff, first on me and then on everyone else.

Okay, then, God does not like the clutter in our heads, so every morning I remove the clutter so I can communicate with God. I do this exercise every morning because I know what I have taken out and handed over back to God and the Universe is pattern and habit. I know it will try to sneak back into my head. So, how do I keep it out? By putting myself on the spot all day long. By asking myself what am I thinking about? If I was practicing doubt, fear, guilt or judgment about anything it was a signal to me to take that thought out of my mind at that very second. It isn't important what I had the doubt about, what is important is that I was practicing doubt or a negative again. When, in the moment, you take out that negative thought, God will reward you with a gift, such as inspiration, wisdom or abundance of some kind. He will see that you put Him first, not the negative. We have to be responsible for every thought that passes through our mind. Our thoughts create our experiences.

So, every morning I hand over the doubt, guilt, fear and judgment. I ask to be present with my mind, in the moment with God. For in the moment is the only place we can communicate with God. I ask myself all day and all night long, 'What am I thinking about, where is my mind? Am I in the moment or is my mind wandering about?' When I am not in the moment I don't communicate with God and I won't get the messages or signs I am to receive from the Universe, God/ Goddess. When that happens, I don't live my life, the precious gift that God gave to me. Life is so short and I really don't want to sleep through any more of it. When you keep the clutter in your head you're in the dead zone.

I believe that God put a circle of light around each one of our souls. That circle is to stay closed to all. It is where we communicate with God. It is where our self-respect and self-preservation exists. Our soul rests in the middle of the circle of light. It is our responsibility in this lifetime to treat our soul with dignity and respect. In that circle of light is where we are, our place to practice that we are. Self-respect, self love, self forgiveness and self kindness; all have to be practiced on ourselves first to know what it feels like, to make it part of our foundation, our DNA. Do not allow anyone to force his or her way into your circle of light and you are not to force yourself into anyone else's circle of light. Do not allow your power to be given away or taken away.

So what do we do with the circle of light where our soul rests? We take it and plop it down in the moment. For in the moment is the only place we can communicate with God. In the moment is God's Funhouse, in the moment is where you have God's confidence. You may not know where you are going but when you take the next step you know you are with God and all will be all right.

Someone once asked me how I got where I am today and I answered, I took a step. I walked into my life and I am still walking.

In the moment we are with God, at peace. What are some of the things that take us away from God?

When we practice doubt, guilt, fear and judgment. Be honest with yourself, check your motivation and your intention. These things take us away from God. You are not in the moment when you practice DOUBT, FEAR, GUILT and JUDGMENT of any kind.

There are a few other things that take us out of the moment. When we dwell in the past and project in the future. God is not in the past nor is He/She in the future. When we compare ourselves to someone else, that is another way of taking ourselves out of the moment and away from God.

We are all unique and God has a definite purpose for all of us. We are not to live each other's lives. We will know God's will when we are in the moment connected to Him. The only real thing in this lifetime is LOVE and God is LOVE.

He has asked us to go within to find Him

and while we do that, He will take care of
the outside for us. I am living proof of that.

Being honest with one's self is hard work,
but worth the trip.

God doesn't like clutter in our heads and
the Angels don't like clutter on the physical
level. It inhibits their entry in. God, Angels
- what a gift to us. We are never alone, ever.

Lenny Spezzano

Table of Contents

DREAMS

Dreams and
Angels go
together,
especially
right now.

Angels are love
and they love
talking to us on
so many levels.
Dreams are a
perfect way for
Angels to
communicate
important messages
to us.
Pay attention to
your Dreams
right now.
Keep a
Dream Journal.

Sometimes you
may wake up
with the feeling
that you have traveled
or received instruction
during your sleep.
Sometimes you wake up
and can't remember
your dreams.
That's where a Dream
Journal will help.
Keep one right
by your bed with
a pen or pencil.
When you wake up in
the morning, before
you fully wake, try
to remember a word or
two from your dreams.

Write down that word
immediately and
as you do,
you will start
to remember
other words and
parts of the dream.
Your dream will unravel
in your memory.
Before you know it
you will have
written down
two or three pages
of information.

It takes practice
and a commitment
on your part
each day to start
to bring down those
dreams to
the Journal.

The Waking State
is half of who we are
and the Dream State
is the other half.
The Dream Journal
is the meeting place
for both States to
come together.
The Dream Journal
becomes a mystical
place for you
and your Angels
to communicate
and connect.

Review your
Dream Journal often
and look for
messages, patterns
and also themes.
Recurrent dreams
are important.
They signify messages
that our Higher Self
and the Angels
are trying to tell us.

Before you go
to sleep at night,
talk to your Angels,
ask them
for protection in
your Dream State.
There are times you
may want to ask
them to help with
a specific situation
that you are
having trouble with.

The Dream State
is a perfect place
to work things out,
a place that is
more comfortable
for you than
your Waking State.

Pay
attention.

Be
aware.

Dreams

Don't forget
to thank your
Guardian Angels
and don't forget
to speak out loud
to them.

Did you know
that ArchAngels
are very accessible
to you,
to help you with
all your needs
and desires?
In another words,
why not call
upon one or two
of them and
ask for
their protection
and assistance during
your dream travel?

Now

Your Angels
are communicating
with you now
to be
in the NOW.
Pay attention
to what is
taking place
in the present.

Don't live
in the past.

Don't always
project into the future.
Learn from
the past,
don't dwell on it.

Move
forward.

We can choose
in the NOW
to take
the steps to
create happiness.
This is
a time for
new beginnings.

NOW means
living in
the moment.

The moment
is the
only place
you can
communicate
with God.

Now

God is
not in
the past
nor is
God in
the future.

God is
in the
present.

Now

In the NOW
is where
we connect
our power
to God's.

What
do you
really feel
NOW?

Now

What
do you
really want
NOW?

What can
you do
NOW to
bring wholeness
into your life?

Start
NOW.

Learn to
say no to
things that
no longer
serve you.

Now

Do not
procrastinate.
Do not
put off
until tomorrow
what needs
to be done
today.

Act in
the NOW
and you
will be a
winner
in the
situation.

You're
with God.
How can
you lose?

NOW
is the only
sure thing
in life.
Make the
most of it.

Learn to see
perfection in
the moment
with a deep
knowingness that
life is unfolding
exactly as
it should

What often
seems like
your worst
disaster
can later
become the best
thing that
ever happened
to you.

See
the perfection
NOW.

Be in
the moment.
Be aware of
situations
surrounding
you NOW.

Look at
the circumstances
of the
present.

Look for
the message
or lesson
and move
forward.

Now

Reach for
the Stars
Angel

How fortunate
we are to
have a visit
from the
"Reach for
the Stars
Angel".

When she
does come,
reach out with
your arms and
welcome her
into your life.

This Angel is
the spirit
of adventure.
"Be bold and
mighty forces will
come to your aid",
is her message.

She says,
"Yes you can!"
when all
the world says,
"Don't be
ridiculous."

This Angel will
help you emerge
without fear
of rejection
and support you
as you risk revealing
who you truly are.
Her essence
encourages you
to express
your thoughts
and feelings freely
as you share
the gift of love.

This Angel is
on her toes,
fully aware and
reaching for the stars.
By her actions
she is fearlessly
manifesting change.

She challenges you
to walk your talk
and dare to dream.
Taking it one step
further this Angel
offers you the choice
to live those dreams.

She will
support you
as you reach
for the stars,
forge new frontiers,
and attain great heights
of awareness.
Peace and enlightenment
right here on Earth
is possible.

She offers you
the chance to
make a difference,
break away
from the mundane
and to
come alive again.

Star Angel

She will
help you to
be all you were
intended to be.
This Reach for
the Stars Angel
sparks the
knowingness with you
that anything
is possible.

What
do you
really feel
NOW?

Invite her
into your life,
embrace her
and don't forget
to say thank you
out loud.

Remember to
stretch
those arms out
and go for it.
If not NOW,
when?

Star Angel

LOOK INTO THE HONEST MIRROR

Me is the word
for now.
This is a time
to look at you
objectively.
Who are you?
Do you know?
Have you given
too much of
yourself away?

Perhaps a
completely new
definition of
yourself
is needed.

Do not be
overly critical.
It is time to pay
attention to
your own
personal needs.
Put yourself first
for a change.
Be you own
best friend.

If you spend
most of your time
rescuing others
perhaps you should
consider what you
are afraid to face
within yourself.
What are you
hiding from?

It may be painful
to allow
the real you
to blossom,
but in the long run
it's ultimately worth
the risk.

Staying forever
lost within
someone else's
expectations is
a high price
to pay for
false security.

Remember ~
you pay
for it
with your life.
Is it
worth it?

Reclaim
your
power.

You hold
within you
amazing potential.
Acknowledge
and use it
for the greatest
and
highest good.

HEALING

This is a time
for healing.
To deal with
emotions and
situations that
have happened
to you in the past
that were
unpleasant and
painful.

This is
a time
to surrender
hurtful emotions
and sadness.

It is a time
to allow
the love
to flow in
and heal
those memories ~
and it is
a time
for forgiveness.

Healing

Do not forget
to forgive
yourself
and the
other
person/persons.

Use this time
for preparation
of what is
to come
in the form
of abundance.

There is
a window of
great opportunity
waiting
for you.

Don't allow
this time
to pass you by –
embrace it
and walk through
with dignity
and anticipation
that the right
and proper actions
will occur.

Healing

You are
not late.

Speak to
your angels
and
ask them
for their help
to walk
with you and
to guide you
through this
most joyous time.

Don't forget
to ask out loud.
And don't forget
to thank
your Angels.
They do deserve
our respect.

SWEETNESS

Sweetness sent
to you
from your
Guardian Angels.

Your
Guardian Angels
are asking you
to notice and
enjoy the nectar
of life.
"You are sweet,"
your Guardian Angel
says of you,
"and I can
help you feel
that happiness and joy."

If you've felt
toughened
by life experiences,
your Angel can
help you lower
your defenses...
and still be safe,
protected
and respected.

This is also
a message
for you to
treat yourself
with tender
sweetness.

Give yourself
rewards and
be kind to
yourself.

Are you
pushing too
hard with
an all work
and no play
approach
to life?

Be a sweetheart
to yourself
and take
some leisure
time to play
and enjoy
the fruits of
your labor.

Your Guardian Angel
will also help you
bring sweetness
into
your relationships
in ways such
as speaking
with love,
acting out
of kindness,
being generous,
giving sincere
compliments and
being thoughtful.

As you show
extra consideration
for others,
it's sure to be
returned to
you plentifully.

Sweetness

God and
the Angels
are helping you
fall back in love
with life
and enjoy
its rich sweetness.

BELIEVE

To heal and
improve
any situation,
it's important
for you
to believe.

To believe
is not easy.
It takes practice
and hard work.

Believing takes
a commitment
with you.

Have faith
in miracles,
the power of
God's healing love
and the
essential goodness
within people.
This is an
important factor
in determining
the outcome
of a situation.

To demonstrate that,
to bring
God's message
to the world,
you must believe
in yourself.

Believe

You are
qualified.
You are ready
and prepared.
You can
do it.

You can
overcome doubt
in yourself
and low opinion
of yourself.

Let go
of worrying
about how
your needs
will be met
because God's
infinite,
creative wisdom
will take care
of the details.

Miracles happen
to you when
you release
and allow God
to take over
and take care
of you.

Believe

Have faith
and put it
into
the practical.

Believe in something
even when
common sense
tells you not to.
Put your
logical mind aside
and trust
your instincts.

Believe

Faith and
Belief live
in your heart,
not in
your mind.

Concentrate on
really knowing
from within.

Believe

Don't allow doubt,
fear, guilt or
judgment to
bring you down.

Let go
and allow God
to take over,
it is how
it was
meant to be.

Don't
fight it.

Let go
and believe
and watch
the miracles
in your life.

TRUTH
TELLER

This message is from
your Guardian Angels.
It is a reminder to you
that it is time to
speak your Truth.
This is a very
strong message
and comes
to you with love.

It is so important
at this time to
speak your truth.
The universe has
openings for
those souls who
are willing to put
their faith in God,
to take that leap
of faith and move
into the unknown.

When the truth
is spoken,
it creates
movement in
the positive.

It creates a place
for God's miracles
and blessings
to be bestowed
upon you

This time,
these openings,
are for you to grow
and move closer
to your Higher Self.
To create more
of an intimacy
with God.

The closer
you are
to God,
the stronger
your connection is
with Him/Her.

It creates
a place to
live your dreams,
to be happy
and be fulfilled
here on earth.

Give any fears
or worries
about others' possible
reaction to God
and your Angels.
You can speak honestly
in a loving way
and still stay
in integrity.

No matter how
others react,
you must give voice
to your truth
as you see it.

Universe, God and
your Angels will
protect you and
will guide your words
as you say them.
All you have to do
is to believe it
and it shall be.

Stick with
what you believe,
regardless of how
people react.

When you speak
the truth
you become
a truth teller,
and as long as
you speak with love
and conviction,
you've got nothing
to fear.

ANGELS AND
GODDESSES

Angels want to
remind us all,
women and men alike,
that it is time to
celebrate the fact
that we are coming out
and we are here
to stay.

Angels &
Goddesses

The Goddess in you
and me is going
through a birth,
a growth and
a spiritual struggle
to grasp that
breath of fresh air.
The fresh air resides
in our homes,
inside of us.
Where the real you
and I are.
Down deep inside.

While we are making
this transformation
into the butterfly,
priestess or healer,
we are not
to be unconscious.
We need to grow,
think and act
for our highest good.
We are to interact
with those around us
we feel spiritually
connected to.

Now,
right now,
more of our
higher purpose
is being shown
to us.
Time will unfold
and fulfill
its purpose.

New happenings
lie in store for us
here on
Mother Earth.
Run, play, laugh
and rejoice.
This is a holy time
and we must honor it,
respect it.
Womanhood
as we know it
is being changed
completely,
180 degrees.

We are
giving birth
to our own
redemption.

Our Angels
play a big part
in this.
They are here
to speak to us,
guide us and be
our partners
during this time.
Our playmates
if you will.

*Angels &
Goddesses*

Remember,
every moment
of everyday,
we are making
choices on what
we want to be.
Someone who is free
or someone that
is enslaved.

The Angels bring
with them lots
of courage for you
and for me.
That is what we need
during this time
of the Goddess.
For we intend
to be different,
to be ourselves,
to be what
God/Goddess wants
us to be and
actually we are
that already,
we just forgot.

*Angels &
Goddesses*

Remember,
inside of us
is what is real,
not the outside.

Love is
the only
real thing,
everything else
is an illusion.

Angels &
Goddesses

I am proud
to be a Goddess
with all who
are around me
these days.
I am blessed.

It has been
too long since
feminine energy has
been felt here
on earth.
Only the Goddess
energy can protect,
heal, intuit, nurture
and endure.

*Angels &
Goddesses*

There has
to be a
balance of man
and woman
here on earth.
Balance is
everything

Equal energy.
Is that so hard
to recognize?

*Angels &
Goddesses*

ANGELS LOVE THE FALL SEASON

Angels sometimes
like to
direct traffic.

Before you perform
any invocation,
decide what spot
or area is the center,
or heart of the situation
or matter.
In other words,
get centered, focus,
grounded and be
connected to
your Higher Self.
If you feel like
your home is
your center,
choose the area
of your home
that seems appropriate.

Once you have
located the center –
even if it is not
a material space
but an inner condition,
sit in perfect silence
and stillness for
a few minutes.

Now,
right now,
more of our
higher purpose
is being shown
to us.
Time will unfold
and fulfill
its purpose.

Now it is time
for you to
raise your arms
and hands towards
the (West),
towards the
(Spirits of Fire).

Say to them,
'I call upon the
Angels of Fire to bring
love, protection,
and safety.
May the warmth of
the life giving fire
come into my being
and guide me.
May the strength
of the sun come to me
and illuminate me
on my way.'

Now it is time
for you to raise
your arms and hands
towards the (North),
towards the
(Spirits of Earth).

Say to them,
'I call upon the
Angels of Earth
to bring love,
protection and safety.
May the regenerative
and restorative power
of the earth
ground me and
guide my way.
May the renewing power
of the moon
come to me
and light my path.'

Now it is time
for you to raise
your arms and hands
towards the (East),
towards the
(Spirits of Air).

Say to them,
'I call upon the
Angels of Air
to bring love,
protection, and safety.
May the gentle winds
of Heaven blow always
and imbue me
with airborne energies.
May the communication
power of Mercury
come to me and
guide my way.'

Now it is time
for you to
raise your arms
and hands towards
the (South),
towards the
(Spirits of Water).

Say to them,
'I call upon the Angels
of water to bring
love, protection
and safety.
May the waters
of Heaven cleanse
and purify me.
May the flowing
and regenerative
powers of water
come to me and
guide my way.'

Go in a
Good Way.

INVITE A GUEST INTO YOUR HOME

Angels love to
be invited into
your home.
Especially when you
have all the clutter
on the physical level
somewhat organized.
Having clutter on
the physical level
inhibits their entry in.
This is a great time
for the partnership
of you and your Angels
to work towards
those miracles you
wanted for so long.
So clean house!

Change of seasons,
like Fall or Spring,
is a time to weed out
what is no longer
of value to you.
Go within to find
what is really important
for your wholeness.
This is a time
for putting together
the pieces of your life.

New directions
and new starts
are here
for you now.
Pay attention to
what is being said
around you.
On all levels,
pay attention.

Your Angels
are helping
the Universe deliver
these messages,
and also they are
here to help you
understand
the messages.

Bringing together
fragmented ideas
or situations can
create a better
understanding of you.
Choose with wisdom.

You could say
that this is a time of
union of broken edges.
The pieces will fit
well with your trust
in yourself.
Ask the Angels
out loud for help
and guidance.
And, of course,
don't forget to
thank them
out loud.

The pieces of
the puzzle are
all there.
Now, you can
put them together
in a
workable form.

Can't wait
to see who
you are!

ARCHANGEL JOPHIEL BRINGS A MESSAGE OF PATIENCE

It takes time for
a seedling to push
through the ground
and mature into
a flower-bearing plant.
Just like a lotus plant
which drops its seeds
into muddy water.
You wonder how
in the world could
such a beautiful flower
come out of all
that mud and dirt.
Yet, each moment
of a plant's life cycle
can bring joy to those
who notice its beauty.

Patience

For those who
choose to stay
in the moment and
not run from it,
miracles will evolve.
Each step is
necessary for
our journey.

Even though we don't
understand it, we must
trust in God, that He/She
knows what's best for us.
As the plant's life cycle
evolves, notice the process
and enjoy watching your
dreams come true. Slow
yourself down and feel
grateful, each step that we
take brings us closer to the
manifestation of miracles
into the practical.
Let's not be asleep
through this process and
notice the lessons with
love, through each action
and situation.

Patience

Archangel Jophiel
supports us in our
everyday life.
Pay attention,
she whispers in our ear
with messages of grace
and peace in our lives.
Grace and peace will
not be noticed if
we do not slow
our minds down to hear.
Imagine applying grace
and peace to your life.

What a difference
that energy will make
in your lives.
Enjoy each moment
and honor it, instead of
projecting in the future.
Whenever you feel
worried or anxious,
call upon Archangel
Jophiel to help you
breathe and slow yourself
down and connect to God.
She will help you increase
your awareness of
yourself and what is
happening around you.
That way you can see and
feel everyday miracles.

Show your respect
and honor Jophiel
by verbally
thanking her
for her gifts
and her presence.

LIFE
PURPOSE

This message is
a reminder that
it is not necessary to
struggle to find
your life purpose.
Don't worry about
how to make
enough money in
a meaningful career.

Don't concern
yourself with quitting
or starting jobs
or professions.
Instead, follow
the path of
your natural desires,
talents and passions
with the full intention
of bringing joy to
yourself and others.

Your life purpose
doesn't need
to be defined
or pinpointed.
It's a process,
not a category.

The purpose of
your life is to serve
in a way that brings
great joy to yourself
and others.
Don't worry about
finding your purpose.
Instead, focus upon
serving a purpose
and then your purpose
will serve you.

Hand over
your worries
about money and career
to God and to
your Angels.
You are on
the right path
towards your
life purpose.
Focus on one step
at a time with respect
to your life's purpose
and release
all your fears
for the future
to your Angels.

What you
are doing
right now
is towards
your life's
purpose.

AFFIRMATIONS FOR ANGELS

I AM (my name) and I AM ready to remember all that I have forgotten. Who I am, why I am here and what I am to do next. I AM READY TO SERVE THE LIGHT! My eyes are fully open to my unique role in this beautiful world.

I AM (my name) and I AM confident and secure in the new direction of my life. I pursue it eagerly and with anticipation of tremendous success. All veils drop away, because I AM READY NOW!

I AM (my name) and I walk through the door of clarity. I leave behind all confusion about who I AM, or what I AM to do next. I choose my actions with confidence. I move forward with courage. And I will always remember the Power that walks beside me.

I AM (my name) and I AM committed to speak the language of TRUTH and JUSTICE and HARMONY at all times. The language of harmony is the true energy of healing. I speak as God would have me speak; with kindness, strength and awareness of the Divine Plan.

I AM (my name) and I AM
determined to overcome any
procrastination that distracts me
from my purpose. I AM committed
to purposeful, direct action in accord
with the laws of my destiny at all
times.

I MOVE FORWARD NOW with
no hesitation!

ABUNDANCE

I allow myself, (my name) in this moment, to be blessed with abundance on all levels; Mental, Spiritual, Physical and Emotional. I am clear in my mind. I am Centered and Balanced. My soul energy is connected to God's. I am strong and confident. I will use all of these gifts for the good of all I come in contact with.

CONSCIOUS AWARENESS

I allow myself, (my name) to grow in conscious awareness and tenderness for my beautiful body now. My body is what God has choosen for me to make a home for Him, inside of me. I honor that, in the home of the presence of God/Goddess. May my deep respect and loving attitude toward my body spark divine light in every cell, energizing me to go forth to help and encourage others.

CROSSING THE THRESHOLD

I allow myself, (my name) to cross the threshold into a new and blessed life as a co-creator with God. I am creating new surroundings and new friends which reflect my dignity and purpose upon the earth.

FREEDOM

The Angels guide you to freely
express your true feelings and
thoughts with Love. Do not hold
back, especially now. It is time
for the Goddess!

ANGELS

Remember to ask your Guardian Angels for help every day, every second of the day.

Their special message for you today is that they are here now for you and they Love you very much. You are never alone. Think of this message as a Love Letter from your Guardian Angels. Our Guardian Angels are God's Divine helpers.

Don't forget to thank them for being in your life.

HELPFUL HINT IN ASKING
FOR WHAT YOU WANT
FROM THE ANGELS

Clear you mind and be in the moment
before you ask out loud your request
from your Angels.

For instance, if you'd like to know
whether you're getting a raise at
work but deep inside you really
want to quit your position and become
self-employed, the Angels will
address your true wishes. You must
be completely and totally honest
about your intentions and motivations
when speaking to the Angels.
You will get what you ask for.

The Great Pizza Pie of Life!

This Pizza Pie has been constructed to help you begin to put balance into your own life. You may wish to change the names of these slices to more realistically mirror the segments of your own life situation.

Each slice is meant to be a segment of your life. Time spent in each slice is not a physical clock; but rather, the clock within yourself. Without equal time spent in each slice, you become unhealthy, uneven, unbalanced. Each slice is essential to your growth and when too much time is spent in one of these slices, you are in danger of the pie tipping over.

Be honest with yourself on your decision on time spent in each slice and be committed to it. It is up to you to take responsibility to move on to the next slice. You must be aware of this in order to accomplish it.

Balance is the Key

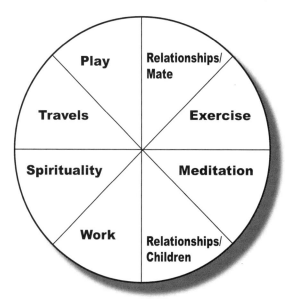

Balance is the Key

*As Life goes on the names
of the slices will change.*